I0016313

Start Building RESTful Microservices using Akka HTTP

Kindle Edition

Ayush Kumar Mishra

Table of Contents

Preface

This book doesn't assume that you are a seasoned software engineer with years of experience in Java, Akka or Akka HTTP. The only prerequisite to this book is that you are "comfortable" with Scala. Scala was selected as the basis for this book attributing to its wide popularity, ease of understanding and learning for those who haven't used it.

This book has been written for developers wanting to start developing REST API right away. I assume you have a basic understanding of Scala. The book does not exhaustively list all feature of Akka HTTP. The writing style of the book saves you the effort of going through long and contrived examples.Each and every topic has been illustrated with a simple to understand example with test-cases. At the end of the book, do find the link to many sample projects, which can also be used as a template.

Even after having a substantial exposure to Akka HTTP, authoring this book was a great learning journey.I hope you enjoy learning Akka HTTP with this book.

About the Author

Ayush Kumar Mishra is a Lead Scala Consultant based in Singapore. He is currently working with Knoldus, an organization where knowledge sharing and upskilling each Knolder is a way of life, which is the only organization to be partners with Lightbend, Databricks, Confluent and Datastax to deliver high-quality reactive products to its global clients. He has been working in Scala for more than 6 years. He is also DataStax certified Cassandra developer. He loves to troubleshoot complex problems and look for the best solutions.

In his career, he has successfully developed and delivered various microservice based systems with Scala, Lagom, Akka HTTP. When he is not programming, he writes technical blogs. Most of his blogs are related to rest API design. He has also transformed some monolithic systems into the microservice based system. He is also the author of **"Start Building RESTful Microservices using Lagom with Scala"**.

Ayush can be contacted the following ways:

Email:- ayush@knoldus.com
LinkedIn:- https://www.linkedin.com/in/ayush-mishra-a2787b23/
Twitter:- https://twitter.com/ayushmishra2005
Facebook:- https://www.facebook.com/ayush.mishra.161

Blog:- https://blog.knoldus.com/author/ayushmishra2005/
GitHub:- https://github.com/ayushmishra2005/

Dedicated To...

This book is dedicated to my wife and to my son, who may be a programmer someday :). Thanks for all their patience, support and love.

Acknowledgments

Special thanks to Pallavi Singh and Sonu Mehrotra for their inputs and feedback as reviewers.

Chapter 1: Introduction

Before you begin reading this book, I just want to elaborate : What is a microservice? Why most big successful applications are moving to microservice architecture and what is needed to make effective microservices?

A microservice is a small composable component that provides a unique business capability. All of us are aware with amazon.com. Now just take it as an example for an instance. We all see it as an e-commerce website but in the background, it is a collection of services that are capable of accepting the orders, providing lists of recommended items, handling of wish lists and managing payments and etal. All these services are micro applications performing a single business capability.

Microservices should not be created around software layers. It means we should not create a web microservice, business logic microservice or database microservice. We should create microservice around business capabilities like order microservice, payment microservice, wishlist microservice and so on. Microservices communicate with each other through a well-defined interface called REST API interface. REST API is known to be stateless, which means if one microservice fails, other microservice should continue to serve the customer.

Some benefits of using microservices:-

1) Smaller code base is easy to maintain.

2) Easy to scale as individual component, that could be released on demand.
3) Push code out to production anytime during the day that's well tested without bringing the system down.

Every microservice is responsible for its own data model and data. They make your application loosely coupled. If you need to upgrade, repair or replace a microservice, we don't need to rebuild entire application. We only need to change the particular microservice.

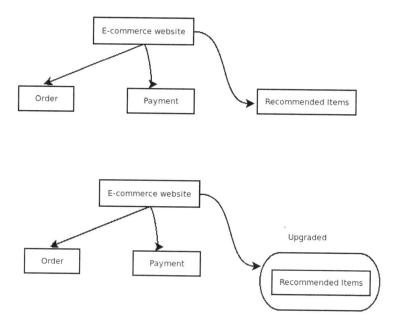

REST APIs are mostly used for building microservices as they are simple and services can communicate with each other over HTTP, without the need of any additional infrastructure.

This book will help you to understand how to build REST API using Akka HTTP and how quickly you can get to speed at building APIs.

What is Akka HTTP?

When you want your application to talk to the external world, you would use HTTP module and Akka HTTP. Akka HTTP is a toolkit for providing and consuming HTTP based web services. As I said, it is a toolkit, so don't consider it as a web framework. It means that if the core of your application is to integrate to the external world, use Akka HTTP otherwise if the core of the application is to interact with the browser then frameworks like Play might be better suited because you would need more things like css, javascript etc.

Akka HTTP provides Fast and Lightweight client and server model which means if your application needs to talk to the external world, you have to use client-side API and if your application is providing service to the external world, you have to use server-side API.

It gives you a powerful DSL for server-side definition. It is fully asynchronous and non-blocking. It included all those nice things with you that you expect from a modern library

It is available for both Java and Scala but in this book, we will go with Scala.

Why Akka HTTP?

Since there are already a lot of scala frameworks to build REST APIs then the obvious question is **Why Akka HTTP?** Let's compare the other scala based frameworks and find out the best use cases for developing with Akka HTTP.

Scalatra

Scalatra is a thread based, Lightweight and complete web framework. As Akka HTTP is built on the top of Akka actor, so actor-model is natural pattern and you won't face any thread safety issue. There might be chances of thread safety issue in Scalatra.

Comparing in terms of performance it has been noted and well established in practice that Akka-http application behaves much better than scalatra and continue to operate well while getting bigger traffic. The efficient performance of Akka HTTP vs Scalatra is largely because of the following :

- Akka Http has better default configurations i.e. thread pool size etc for optimal performance.
- Akka Http is fully integrated into Typesafe stack.
- Akka Http allows database connection pool to expand and scale out more efficiently for better throughput.

Spray

It was the one that worked in akka style to build api's. As it was heavily dependent on the implementation of Akka Actors and its ecosystem.

There are some issues with Spray, which have been resolved in Akka HTTP for example:

1) Dealing with large message entities can be difficult in Spray because it doesn't have a proper stream abstraction. As Akka HTTP is built on the top of Akka stream that resolves this problem in a nice manner.
2) Some feature like websocket support is missing in Spray but included in Akka HTTP.

Akka HTTP is similar to Spray 2.0 so it's not something entirely different but it's really the natural improvement, which addresses the weaknesses of Spray. It also has Java API so you should be able to use Akka HTTP with Java completely with all its features which were impossible in Spray because Spray was completely in Scala.

Play
It is full stack web framework. It's stable, very well designed, extremely well documented. So if you have UI in use , Play is a good choice.But if you don't need to have a UI probably going with Akka HTTP is the best choice.

Modules of Akka HTTP
Akka HTTP is structured into several modules:

akka-http-core
A complete low-level server- and client-side implementation of HTTP such as a connection, WebSockets etc. It implements HTTP "essentials" with no high-level features.

akka-http

Higher-level functionality such as (un)marshalling, (de)compression as well as a powerful DSL for defining HTTP-based APIs on the server-side.

akka-http-testkit

A set of utilities for verifying server-side service implementations.

akka-http-spray-json

Predefined glue-code for (de)serializing custom types from/to JSON with spray-json. It is possible to use Akka HTTP with other JSON serializers.

akka-http-xml

Predefined glue-code for (de)serializing custom types from/to XML with scala-xml.

Chapter 2: Start with Akka HTTP

To start with Akka HTTP, we have to include 3 libraries.

You should add the following dependency to the project. I am using sbt here. You can also use other build tools like maven or gradle.

```
// For Akka 2.4.x or 2.5.x
"com.typesafe.akka" %% "akka-http" % "10.0.10"


// At the time of writing this book, the latest version was
"10.0.10", you can go Akka HTTP official website to include
the latest version.

// Only when running against Akka 2.5 explicitly depend
on akka-streams in same version as akka-actor
"com.typesafe.akka" %% "akka-stream" % "2.5.4" // or
whatever the latest version is
"com.typesafe.akka" %% "akka-actor"  % "2.5.4" // or
whatever the latest version is
```

If you are using any other build tool, you can include libraries in corresponding build tool style.

Chapter 3: Configuration

Since it is fully integrated into the Typesafe stack, so it's easy to use same kind of configuration for your application. Akka HTTP provides default values for its modules to start development.

akka-http-core: This contains configuration parameters for a low-level implementation, for both client and server APIs

akka-http: This contains configuration parameters for a high-level implementation. Currently, it is the Routing DSL configuration.

To find out all configuration parameters with their value, refer here *https://doc.akka.io/docs/akka-http/current/scala/http/configuration.html*

How to override default values:

If you want to change default behavior or want to define application-specific settings, as with Akka-related projects, the configuration needs to be defined in the Typesafe configuration file *application.conf*.

Let's see how to modify the parameters.

server.request-timeout:- The default value is 20 seconds. If the application is taking a long time to produce a response, 20 seconds might not be enough.

max-content-length:- Default value is 8 minutes. If your application is supposed to run in an embedded device, large requests might not be acceptable.

uri-parsing-mode:- Default value is strict. If you want to allow all 7-Bit ASCII chars in url, you might need to change this.

illegal-header-warnings:- By default it is turned on. If your application is getting many invalid headers and you want to turn off logging of the warning message, you can turn off it.

client.connecting-timeout:- The default value is 10 seconds. If the server is slow for any reason like taking too much time for connecting to the database, 10 seconds might not be enough.

akka.http.parsing sets that configuration for both the server and client. However, it is possible to just set different parameters for each server and client. To do so, we need to set either *akka.http.server.parsing* or *akka.http.client.parsing*

```
akka.http {
    server.request-timeout = 60s
    parsing.max-content-length = 1m
    parsing.uri-parsing-mode = relaxed
    client.connecting-timeout = 60s
    parsing.uri-parsing-mode = off
  }

In the default parameter list, you will see something like below:
```

```
# Modify to tweak parsing settings on the server-side only.
  parsing {
    # no overrides by default, see `akka.http.parsing` for
default values
  }

Or

# Modify to tweak parsing settings on the client-side only.
  parsing {
    # no overrides by default, see `akka.http.parsing` for
default values
  }
```

.

Chapter 4: HTTP model of Akka HTTP

HTTP model is very similar to what we have in the spray. It's High-level abstraction for most things that you work with in HTTP. It gives you the core types such as predefined common media types, status codes etc. It is also open to extension. All the components of HTTP data structure are available in *akka-http-core* library. HTTP model in Akka HTTP is fully immutable and case class based data model.
By importing following, you can use them in your code:-

import akka.http.scaladsl.model._

HttpRequest

The immutable HTTP request model consists of:-

```
//All parameters of HttpRequest model have default
values set.
case class HttpRequest(
 method: HttpMethod = HttpMethods.GET,
 uri: Uri = Uri./,
 headers: immutable.Seq[HttpHeader] = Nil,
 entity: RequestEntity = HttpEntity.Empty,
 protocol: HttpProtocol = HttpProtocols.`HTTP/1.1`
) extends HttpMessage

//HttpRequest samples
val default = HttpRequest()

val sample1 = HttpRequest(uri = "/users")

val sample2 = HttpRequest(POST, uri = "/users",
```

```
entity = ByteString("User1"))

val sample3 = HttpRequest(
 PUT,
 uri = "/users",
 entity = HttpEntity(`text/plain` withCharset `UTF-
8`, ByteString("User2")),
 headers = List(mHeaders.Allow(POST, PUT),
mHeaders.Authorization(BasicHttpCredentials("user",
"pass"))),
 protocol = `HTTP/1.0`)
```

HttpResponse

The immutable HTTP response model consists of:-

```
//All parameters of HttpResponse model have default
values set.
case class HttpResponse(
 status: StatusCode = StatusCodes.OK,
 headers: immutable.Seq[HttpHeader] = Nil,
 entity: ResponseEntity = HttpEntity.Empty,
 protocol: HttpProtocol = HttpProtocols.`HTTP/1.1`
) extends HttpMessage

//HttpResponse samples
val default = HttpResponse(200)

val sample1 =
HttpResponse(StatusCodes.OK,List(),HttpEntity(Conte
ntType(MediaTypes.`application/json`),
"""[]"""),HttpProtocols.`HTTP/1.1`)
```

Example with test-cases can be found here:-
https://gist.github.com/ayushmishra2005/46068d96af10ef4
911aba8c9fbb1bc63

HttpEntity

Akka HTTP provides 5 different types of entities:-

1) HttpEntity.Strict

```
case class Strict(contentType: ContentType, data:
ByteString) extends UniversalEntity
```

The Strict entity is a `UniversalEntity`, which you can use anywhere. But it's not the most general one.
This is the simplest form of entity, which is used when an entity is small unchunked HTTP message with fixed data and loaded completely in memory.

2) HttpEntity.Default

```
case class Default(contentType: ContentType,
contentLength: Long,
data: Source[ByteString]) extends UniversalEntity
```

This is the most general entity. This is used when an entity is unchunked HTTP message with a known length, which is generated by a streaming data source. Content length must be non-zero positive. For empty entities, you can use `HttpEntity.empty(contentType)`.

3) HttpEntity.Chunked

```
case class Chunked(contentType: ContentType,
```

```
chunks: Source[ChunkStreamPart]) extends
MessageEntity
```

In the Chunked entity, there is no content-length because the chunked message has no content-length header. It extends MessageEntity which means you can use it in requests and responses but not in the body part. This is used when data is sent in a series of chunks by setting 'Transfer-Encoding' header as 'chunked'. It is useful when larger amounts of data are sent to the client and the total size of the response may not be known until the request has been fully processed. An element of the HttpEntity data stream can be either a `Chunk` or a `LastChunk`. `LastChunk` is optional and can be used to terminate the stream.

4) HttpEntity.CloseDelimited:-

```
case class CloseDelimited(contentType: ContentType,
data: Source[ByteString]) extends ResponseEntity
```

CloseDelimited extends ResponseEntity, which means you can use it only on responses, not on requests. This is used for unchunked data with an unknown length. It is implicitly delimited by closing the connection. This type of HttpEntity can only be used for HttpResponses because connection must be closed after sending a response. It is used only for specific scenarios for ex: If an entity doesn't support chunked transfer encoding, we can use this type of entity.

We should avoid using this type of entity because it degrades the performance since it prevents connection reuse, use HttpEntity.Chunked instead.

5) HttpEntity.IndefiniteLength

```
case class IndefiniteLength(contentType:
ContentType, data: Source[ByteString]) extends
BodyPartEntity
```

It is used when there is a streaming entity of a BodyPart with an indefinite length. This type of HttpEntity can only be used for BodyParts.

Note

1. First three subtypes of HttpEntity can be used for both request and response. But *HttpEntity.CloseDelimited* can only be used for responses.
2. Streaming entity types (i.e. all but Strict) cannot be shared or serialized. We can use *HttpEntity.toStrict* to create a strict, shareable copy of an entity.

3. If we want special handling for any of the subtype, we can do pattern match over the subtypes of HttpEntity.

4. There is HttpEntity companion object, which provides several factory methods to create entities from common types easily.

5. There is length verification check, which gets automatically attached to all message entities that Akka HTTP reads from the network. This checks that the total entity size is less than or equal to the configured

max-content-length(akka.http.parsing.max-content-length (applying to server- as well as client-side), akka.http.server.parsing.max-content-length (server-side only), akka.http.client.parsing.max-content-length (client-side only) or akka.http.host-connection-pool.client.parsing.max-content-length (only host-connection-pools)).

This is a global limit for all request and responses. To override this property for a particular request, you can use withSizeLimit method of HttpEntity. We use this limit for defending your network against certain Denial-of-Service attacks.

Examples

```
HttpRequest(entity =
HttpEntity.Default(ContentTypes.`text/plain(UTF-
8)`, 100, Source.empty))

HttpResponse(
  entity = HttpEntity.CloseDelimited(
    ContentTypes.`text/plain(UTF-8)`,
    Source.single(ByteString("Foo"))))

HttpRequest(
  entity = HttpEntity.Chunked(
    ContentTypes.`text/plain(UTF-8)`,
    Source(List(HttpEntity.Chunk(ByteString("Foo")),
HttpEntity.LastChunk("foo=bar", List(Age(30),
RawHeader("Cache-Control", "public"))))))))
```

HTTP Header model

In Akka HTTP, all request and response headers are modeled using case classes. Akka HTTP will receive all type of valid/invalid headers as long as message as a whole is valid.

If a header is valid, it will get parsed into its respective model classes automatically otherwise a parsing error will be logged depending on the value configured as in below config settings.

```
# If a header cannot be parsed into a high-level model
instance it will be
   # provided as a `RawHeader`.
   # If logging is enabled it is performed with the
configured
   # `error-logging-verbosity`.
   illegal-header-warnings = on

   # Configures the verbosity with which message (request
or response) parsing
   # errors are written to the application log.
   #
   # Supported settings:
   # `off`  : no log messages are produced
   # `simple`: a condensed single-line message is logged
   # `full`  : the full error details (potentially spanning
several lines) are logged
   error-logging-verbosity = full

   # Configures the processing mode when encountering
illegal characters in
```

```
# header value of response.
#
# Supported mode:
# `error`  : default mode, throw an ParsingException and
terminate the processing
# `warn`   : ignore the illegal characters in response
header value and log a warning message
# `ignore` : just ignore the illegal characters in response
header value
  illegal-response-header-value-processing-mode = error
```

Invalid headers will be transformed into RawHeader
instances.

Valid Headers Example

```
Authorization(BasicHttpCredentials("user", "pass"))

Location("http://example.com/")
```

Custom HTTP Model

HTTP model in Akka Http is open for extension, means
you can model custom headers, custom media types,
custom status codes and custom HTTP methods.

Custom Headers

You can create custom headers by extending
ModeledCustomHeader or *CustomHeader*.
ModeledCustomHeader is less painful as compared to
CustomHeader and is also preferred because you can
match a *ModeledCustomHeader* against a *RawHeader* or
the other way around.

```scala
final class ApiTokenModeledHeader(token: String)
extends ModeledCustomHeader[ApiTokenModeledHeader]
{
 override def renderInRequests = false
 override def renderInResponses = false
 override val companion = ApiTokenModeledHeader
 override def value: String = token
}
object ApiTokenModeledHeader extends
ModeledCustomHeaderCompanion[ApiTokenModeledHeader]
{
 override val name = "apiKey"
 override def parse(value: String) = Try(new
ApiTokenModeledHeader(value))
}

case class ApiTokenHeader(token: String) extends
CustomHeader {
 override def renderInRequests = false
 override def renderInResponses = false
 override def value: String = token
 override val name = "apicustomKey"
}


"A custom header" should "be validated" in {
 val ApiTokenModeledHeader(t1) =
ApiTokenModeledHeader("token")
 t1 should ===("token")

 val RawHeader(k2, v2) =
ApiTokenModeledHeader("token")
 k2 should ===("apiKey")
 v2 should ===("token")

 // will match, header keys are case insensitive
 val ApiTokenModeledHeader(v3) =
RawHeader("APIKEY", "token")
 v3 should ===("token")

 intercept[MatchError] {
 // won't match, different header name
 val ApiTokenModeledHeader(v6) =
```

```
RawHeader("different", "token")
}

 val ApiTokenHeader(v4) = ApiTokenHeader("token")
 v4 should ===("token")

 // Will not compile
 /*val ApiTokenHeader(v5) =
RawHeader("APICUSTOMKEY", "token")
 v5 should ===("token") */
}
```

You can find the complete example here:-
https://gist.github.com/ayushmishra2005/f9d85da71e
6d654ec7d495269f0bcb99

Custom Media Types

You can also define custom media types by creating
ParserSettings with *withCustomMediaTypes* method and
then register ParserSettings in ServerSettings using
withParserSettings method.

```
val parserSettings =
ParserSettings(system).withCustomMediaTypes(`applic
ation/mediacustom`)

val serverSettings =
ServerSettings(system).withParserSettings(parserSet
tings)
```

Custom Status Code

Similarl to custom media types, you can also define
custom status codes by creating *ParserSettings* with
withCustomStatusCodes method and then register
ParserSettings in *ServerSettings* using *withParserSettings*
method.

```
val customCode = StatusCodes.custom(111,
"customCode", "Reason for this custom code",
isSuccess = true, allowsEntity = false)

val parserSettings =
ParserSettings(system).withCustomStatusCodes(custom
Code)
val serverSettings =
ServerSettings(system).withParserSettings(customCod
e)
```

Custom HTTP Method

Similarly to custom media types, you can also define custom http method by creating *ParserSettings* with *withCustomMethods* method and then registering *ParserSettings* in *ServerSettings* using *withParserSettings* method.

```
val PULL = HttpMethod.custom("PULL", safe = false,
idempotent = true, requestEntityAcceptance =
Expected)

val parserSettings =
ParserSettings(system).withCustomMethods(PULL)

val serverSettings =
ServerSettings(system).withParserSettings(parserSet
tings)
```

Chapter 5: URI model of Akka HTTP

URI model in Akka HTTP is a fully immutable, case class-based data model. Since Akka HTTP follows **RFC 3986** protocol to define URI syntax, hence it's URI model contains five components *scheme, authority, path, query, and fragment.*

```
case class Uri(
  scheme: String,
  authority: Authority,
  path: Path,
  rawQueryString: Option[String],
  fragment: Option[String]
)
```

In the below example, you can see how these five components are extracted from a Uri string.

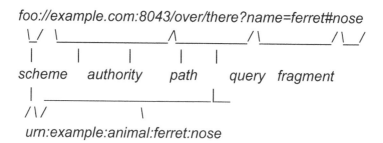

There are different ways to construct the instance of Uri case class:-

```
Uri("foo://example.com:8043/over/there?name=ferret#
nose")
    •   //akka.http.scaladsl.model.Uri =
        foo://example.com:8043/over/there?name=ferre
```

```
      t#nose

Uri.from(scheme = "foo", host = "example.com", port
= 8043,
  path = "/over/there", queryString =
Some("name=ferret"), fragment =  Some("nose"))
//akka.http.scaladsl.model.Uri =
foo://example.com:8043/over/there?name=ferret#nose

Uri("mailto:ayush@example.com")
//akka.http.scaladsl.model.Uri =
mailto:ayush@example.com

Uri.from(scheme = "tel", path = "+1-23-111-1212")
//akka.http.scaladsl.model.Uri = tel:+1-23-111-1212

If we try to parse a URI, which is not valid
according to RFC 3986, we will get
IllegalUriException.

Uri("foö:/a")
//akka.http.scaladsl.model.IllegalUriException: Illegal URI
reference: Invalid input 'ö', expected scheme-char, 'EOI',
'#', ':', '?', slashSegments or pchar (line 1, column 3): foö:/a
```

Special character handling in Query string:-

Uri.query method is used to parse raw query string into *Query* instance. This method takes parsing mode as one of the argument. There are two parsing modes available in Uri model: *Uri.ParsingMode.Strict* and *Uri.ParsingMode.Relaxed*. The default value of this argument in *Uri.query* method is *Uri.ParsingMode.Relaxed*.

You can also specify the mode in configuration as well:
uri-parsing-mode = strict

There may be special characters in the query string, which may be percent-encoded or not. If we use Strict mode to parse the query, it will not allow some special characters without percent-encoded. It will throw ***IllegalUriException*** for those special characters. We can allow these special characters by using Relaxed mode.

However "/" and "?" are allowed in query string without needs to be percent-encoded because According to RFC 3986 standard,

The characters slash ("/") and question mark ("?") may represent data within the query component.

Here are some examples:-

```
val uri = Uri.from(scheme = "foo", host =
"example.com", port = 8043, path = "/over/there",
queryString = Some("a=^1&a=2&a=3&b=4^"))

uri.query().toMultiMap
//Map(a -> List(^1, 2, 3), b -> List(4^))

uri.query(mode = Uri.ParsingMode.Strict).toMultiMap
/* akka.http.scaladsl.model.IllegalUriException:
Illegal query:
Invalid input '^', expected pchar, '&' or 'EOI'
(line 1, column 3): a=^1&a=2&a=3&b=4^
*/
```

Now if we make this special character percent-encoded in above example, it will be allowed even if mode is Strict:

```
val uri = Uri.from(scheme = "foo", host =
"example.com", port = 8043,
path = "/over/there", queryString =
Some("a=%5E1&a=2&a=3&b=4%5E"))
```

```
uri.query(mode = Uri.ParsingMode.Strict).toMultiMap
//Map(a -> List(^1, 2, 3), b -> List(4^))
```

There are also some special characters, which will not be allowed in either of the modes if they are not percent-encoded.

```
val uri = Uri.from(scheme = "foo", host =
"example.com", port = 8043,
path = "/over/there", queryString = Some("a=#1"))

uri.query().toMultiMap
//akka.http.scaladsl.model.IllegalUriException:
Illegal query: Invalid input '#', expected part,
'&' or 'EOI' (line 1, column 3): a=#1

uri.query(mode = Uri.ParsingMode.Strict).toMultiMap
//akka.http.scaladsl.model.IllegalUriException:
Illegal query: Invalid input '#', expected part,
'&' or 'EOI' (line 1, column 3): a=#1
```

However, you can still get the value of *queryString* by *Uri.rawQueryString* method.

```
val uri = Uri.from(scheme = "foo", host =
"example.com", port = 8043,
path = "/over/there", queryString = Some("a=#1"))

uri.rawQueryString
//Some(a=#1)
```

You can find example here:
https://gist.github.com/ayushmishra2005/6c425733394
8773489736b84d7cf54e2

Chapter 6: JSON (un)marshalling support

Before starting to work on your application, you must know the following.

- How would you get and use the wire format data of request/response body in your application?
- How would you convert back your application object into over the wire format, so that it could be sent down a wire?

We use *Marshalling* and *Unmarshalling* for transforming request and response bodies between the-wire formats and objects.

Marshalling is the process of converting it into a form suitable for serialized storage or transmission, converting higher-level (object) into a form that could be sent down a wire. For ex: Converting an object into JSON.

Unmarshalling is the other side of this process. It is the process of converting a wire format data into a higher-level (object).

Marshalling/Unmarshalling is similar to *Serialization/Deserialization* except for few differences:
1) Marshalling is different from serialization in that marshalling treats remote objects specially.

2) Marshalling implies moving the data, it does not imply transforming the data from its native representation or storage. Serializing implies transforming the data to some

non-native intermediate representation.

3) Serializing an object means to convert its state into a byte stream in such a way that the byte stream can be converted back into a copy of the object.
Marshalling an object means to record its state and codebase(s) in such a way that when the marshalled object is "unmarshalled," a copy of the original object is obtained, possibly by automatically loading the class definitions of the object.

In this tutorial, my focus would be more on *json-support* rather than *xml-support*.

In Akka Http, We use **spray-json** library, which is provided by **akka-http-spray-json** module, to marshal/Unmarshal JSON object. Add this in your project:

"com.typesafe.akka" %% "akka-http-spray-json" % "10.0.10"

Note: At the time, when this book was written, the current version was *10.0.10*. You must check the current version before implementing in your project.
spray-json is a lightweight, clean and efficient JSON parser. *spray-json* comes with a *DefaultJsonProtocol*, which already covers all of Scala's value types as well as the most important reference and collection types.

As long as your code uses nothing more than these you only need the *DefaultJsonProtocol*. Here are the types already taken care of by the *DefaultJsonProtocol*:

- Byte, Short, Int, Long, Float, Double, Char, Unit, Boolean
- String, Symbol
- BigInt, BigDecimal
- Option, Either, Tuple1 - Tuple7
- List, Array
- immutable.{Map, Iterable, Seq, IndexedSeq, LinearSeq, Set, Vector}
- collection.{Iterable, Seq, IndexedSeq, LinearSeq, Set}
- JsValue

But for any custom type T, you have to use *JsonFormat[T]*:

```scala
case class Employee(id: String, name: String)
case class Employees(employees: Seq[Employee])

trait JsonSupport extends SprayJsonSupport {

  import DefaultJsonProtocol._
  implicit val employeeJsonFormat =
jsonFormat2(Employee)
  implicit val employeessJsonFormat =
jsonFormat1(Employees)
}
```

SprayJsonSupport is a trait providing automatic to and from JSON marshalling/unmarshalling using an in-scope spray-json protocol. Since the marshalling/Unmarshalling infrastructure of Akka HTTP relies on a type-class based approach, so Marshaller/UnMarshaller have to be available implicitly.

For regular class, there is a different way to do this.

```scala
class Employee(val name: String)
object MyJsonProtocol extends DefaultJsonProtocol {
  implicit object ColorJsonFormat extends
```

```
RootJsonFormat[Employee] {
    def write(c: Employee) =
      JsArray(JsString(c.name))

    def read(value: JsValue) = value match {
      case JsArray(Vector(JsString(name))) =>
        new Employee(name)
      case _ => deserializationError("Employee
expected")
    }
  }
}
```

You can find complete example here:-

https://gist.github.com/ayushmishra2005/7f159b57f14a14afe6a34f1ffee20383

Chapter 7: Server-Side API Implementation

Akka HTTP server side gives you support for fully asynchronous *HTTP/1.1*, where all connections are considered persistent. They allow multiple requests to use a single connection. Basically, there is a single TCP connection to send and receive multiple HTTP requests/responses, as opposed to opening a new connection for every single request/response pair. It uses HTTP pipelining to send multiple HTTP requests on a single TCP connection without waiting for the corresponding responses.

It also provides a simple API to implement services using WebSocket to provide full-duplex communication channels over a single TCP connection.

Akka HTTP provides two ways to implement Server-side API:

Low-Level Server-Side API
High-Level Server-Side API

In this book, we will be focusing more on High-Level Server-Side API, since this is the recommended way to write HTTP servers with Akka HTTP. That's why I will give only a small overview of Low-Level Server-Side API. You can choose either of the implementation based on your need.

Low-Level Server-Side API

akka-http-core module provides an implementation for low-level API. It contains all core and essential features of the HTTP server. For ex: Accepting incoming connection, handling HTTP request and responding them through HTTP response. All non-core functionalities are provided by ***akka-http*** module, which is being used for higher-level API.

First, we would need to bind the server on a given endpoint.

val serverSource = Http().bind(interface = host, port = port)

We are passing interface and port in *Http().bind* method to get the incoming connection to be accepted, which will be published as *Http.IncomingConnection*. This method also accepts other arguments. We can set them according to our needs. If no port is provided, default post **80** will be set for HTTP and **443** for HTTPS. Http.IncomingConnection provides methods to handle requests coming in over this connection.

Let's see a complete example of Low-Level Server-Side

```
trait LowLevelAPIRoutes {

  implicit val system = ActorSystem()
  implicit val materializer = ActorMaterializer()
  lazy val log = Logging(system,
classOf[LowLevelAPIRoutes])

  val requestHandler: HttpRequest => HttpResponse =
{
    case HttpRequest(GET, Uri.Path("/"), _, _, _) =>
```

```
      HttpResponse(entity = HttpEntity(
        ContentTypes.`text/html(UTF-8)`,
        "<html><body>Hello!</body></html>"
      ))

   case r: HttpRequest =>
     r.discardEntityBytes()
     HttpResponse(404, entity = "Unknown
resource!")
 }
}

object LowLevelServerAPISample extends App with
LowLevelAPIRoutes {
 implicit val executionContext = system.dispatcher
 val host = "localhost"
 val port = 8080
 val serverSource = Http().bind(interface = host,
port = port)

 val bindingFuture: Future[Http.ServerBinding] =
   serverSource.to(Sink.foreach { connection =>
     println("Accepted new connection from " +
connection.remoteAddress)
     connection handleWithSyncHandler
requestHandler
   }).run()

 bindingFuture.failed.foreach { ex =>
   log.error(ex, "Failed to bind to {}:{}!", host,
port)
 }
}
```

As you can see in *LowLevelAPIRoutes*, we have defined a partial function *requestHandler*, which is transforming HttpRequest into HttpResponse.

```
case HttpRequest(GET, Uri.Path("/"), _, _, _) =>
  HttpResponse(entity = HttpEntity(
  ContentTypes.`text/html(UTF-8)`,
  "<html><body>Hello!</body></html>"
  ))
```

Here we are doing a pattern match over the incoming HttpRequest. We can also pass other parameters in *HttpRequest* such as *HttpHeader*, HttpEntity or HttpProtocol to handle a particular request according to our requirement. Above code does not look very convenient to create request handlers. That's why High-Level Server-Side is a recommended way to write routes because it uses powerful and more flexible "**Routing DSL**" to write routes instead of inspecting requests and creating responses manually..

In this above example, we have used *handleWithSyncHandler* to handle the requests. However, we can also call *handleWithAsyncHandler* or *handleWith*. You can choose according to your requirement.

There are some scenarios, when failures may occur. By default, Akka will log all these failures but one can also perform any action in case of server failure instead of just being logged them.

```
bindingFuture.failed.foreach { ex => log.error(ex,
"Failed to bind to {}:{}!", host, port)
}
```

You can find complete example here:-
https://gist.github.com/ayushmishra2005/162109cd525 f3f095c2c78363376052c

High-Level Server-Side API

As we have seen the previous example of *low-level server-side* API, this approach is not developer friendly and also very inconvenient for the big application. It doesn't help in keeping your API implementation as DRY as you might like.

Akka HTTP provides a powerful, very flexible feature called
"**Routing DSL**" for defining the layout of your REST API as
a structure of composable elements in a concise and
readable way. These composable elements are called
"**Directives**". Directives are functions that either let the
HTTP request through or reject it depending on its nature.

Since it provides the higher-level functionality of typical
web servers or frameworks, like deconstruction of URIs,
content negotiation,(un)marshalling, (de)compression as
well as a powerful DSL for defining HTTP-based APIs on
the server-side, hence it is called *High-Level Server-Side
implementation*.

akka-http module is being used to provide these Higher-
level functionalities. This is the recommended way to write
HTTP servers with Akka HTTP. Routing DSL describes
HTTP "*routes*" and their handling.

Each route is composed of one or more level of *Directive*
that narrows down to handling one specific type of request.
We will read Directive in next chapter in detail.

Let's see an example

```scala
case class Employee(id: String, name: String)
case class Employees(employees: Seq[Employee])

trait JsonSupport extends SprayJsonSupport {

  import DefaultJsonProtocol._

  implicit val employeeJsonFormat =
jsonFormat2(Employee)
```

```scala
 implicit val employeessJsonFormat =
jsonFormat1(Employees)
}


trait EmployeeRoutes extends JsonSupport {
 implicit def system: ActorSystem

 lazy val log = Logging(system,
classOf[EmployeeRoutes])
 var list: Employees = Employees(Nil)
 implicit lazy val timeout = Timeout(5.seconds)

 lazy val employeeRoutes: Route =
   pathPrefix("employees") {
     pathEnd {
       get {
         complete(list)
       } ~
         post {
           entity(as[Employee]) { employee =>
             list = list.copy(employees =
list.employees ++ Seq(employee))
             log.info("Created employee :",
employee.name)
             complete((StatusCodes.Created,
employee))
           }
         }
     }
   }
}

object ServerStarter extends App with
EmployeeRoutes {
 implicit val system = ActorSystem("my-system")
 implicit val materializer = ActorMaterializer()
 implicit val executionContext = system.dispatcher

 val (host, port) = ("localhost", 8080)
 val bindingFuture: Future[ServerBinding] =
   Http().bindAndHandle(employeeRoutes, host, port)

 log.info(s"Server online at
http://localhost:8080/\nPress RETURN to stop...")
 bindingFuture.failed.foreach { ex =>
   log.error(ex, "Failed to bind to {}:{}!", host,
port)
```

```
    }
  }
```

As you can see from above example, the way of writing routes is more concise and readable as compared to Low-Level Server-Side api implementation. In the above example, *employeeRoutes* is a Route which is constructed by nesting various directives which route an incoming request to the appropriate handler block. This is a simple example to give you a feel for what an actual API definition with the Routing DSL will look like.

You can find complete example here:
https://gist.github.com/ayushmishra2005/7f159b57f14a14afe6a34f1ffee20383

Routes

There are few important things to know about Routes.

1) It is the main component of Akka HTTP's *Routing DSL*.

```
type Route = RequestContext => Future[RouteResult]
```

It converts RequestContext into a *Future[RouteResult]*.

2) *RequestContext* wraps *HttpRequest* with additional informations that are typically required by the routing logic, like an *ExecutionContext* etc. It also contains some helper methods which allow for the convenient creation of modified copies.

3) *RouteResult* is a sealed trait and inherited by two final case classes: *Complete* and *Rejected*

4) After receiving a request, route calls "*complete*" method and a given response is sent to the client as a reaction to the request. It can also reject the request by calling "*reject*" method.

5) You can create Route chaining by composing routes with the concatenation operator ~, which is an extension method that becomes available when you *import akka.http.scaladsl.server.Directives._*. This is useful for building more complex routes from simpler ones.

6) *Route.seal* is used to wrap a route with default exception handling and rejection conversion. If you bring implicit rejection and/or exception handlers to the top-level scope, your route is sealed.
Route.seal() is used to perform modification on HttpResponse from the route.

```
respondWithHeader (RawHeader ("special-header", "Your
header is modified.")) {
  Route.seal (pathPrefix ("employees") {
    pathEnd {
      get { ctx =>
        ctx.complete (list)
      }
    }
  })
}
```

Chapter 8: Directives

Directives are composable elements that creates routes.

Example

```
pathEnd {
 get {
   complete(list)
 }
}
```

You can also write code as:

```
pathEnd {
 get { ctx =>
   ctx.complete(list)
 }
}
```

Last one is written as an explicit function literal.

The directive makes the code more concise, readable and maintainable. Akka HTTP's Routing DSL you should almost never have to fall back to creating routes via Route function literals that directly manipulate the RequestContext.

Structure of a directive is similar to:

```
name(arguments) { extractions =>
  ... // inner route
}
```

arguments and inner route are optional. Directives can "extract" a number of values and make them available to their inner routes as function arguments.

According to Akka HTTP official documentation, A directive can do one or more of the following:

1. Transform the incoming *RequestContext* before passing it on to its inner route (i.e. modify the request)
2. Filter the *RequestContext* according to some logic, i.e. only pass on certain requests and reject others
3. Extract values from the *RequestContext* and make them available to its inner route as "extractions"
4. Chain some logic into the *RouteResult* future transformation chain (i.e. modify the response or rejection)
5. Complete the request

Let's see an example:

```
val routes = {
  path("contacts") {
    parameter('name) { name =>
      complete {
        findByName(name).map {
          case Some(result) => HttpResponse(entity =
write(result))
          case None => HttpResponse(entity = "This
contact does not exist")
        }
      }
    }
  }
}
```

In the above example, This URL *"/contacts?name=foo"* will get the data on the basis of the query parameter. Here one thing is to note that the argument to the complete directive is evaluated by-name, it means it is re-evaluated every time the produced route is run.

Composing Directives

There are many ways to compose directives:-

1) ~(tilde)

```
path("employee" / IntNumber) { id =>
 get {
   complete {
     "Received GET request for employee " + id
   }
 } ~
   put {
     complete {
       "Received PUT request for employee " + id
     }
   }
}
```

2) *concat* Combinator

```
def innerRoute(id: Int): Route =
 concat(get {
   complete {
     "Received GET request for employee " + id
   }
 },
   put {
     complete {
       "Received PUT request for employee " + id
     }
   })

lazy val employeeRoutes: Route =
 path("employee" / IntNumber) { id =>
innerRoute(id) }
```

3) | operator

```
lazy val employeeRoutes: Route =
```

```
path("employee" / IntNumber) { id =>
   (get | put) { ctx =>
     ctx.complete(s"Received
${ctx.request.method.name} request for employee
$id")
   }
}
```

4) **&** operator

```
val employeeGetOrPutWithMethod =
 path("employee" / IntNumber) & (get | put) &
extractMethod

val employeeRoutes =
 employeeGetOrPutWithMethod { (id, m) =>
   complete(s"Received ${m.name} request for
employee $id")
 }
```

As I have already mentioned at the starting of the book, the aim of this book is to provide that kind of knowledge, which you can use to quickly start development in Akka HTTP.

Akka HTTP has a huge collection of predefined directives. We will focus only on most commonly used directives. Akka HTTP also gives you the flexibility to write custom directive.

There are two types of directives:-

Directives filtering or extracting from the request
Directives creating or transforming the response

Let's focus on the first one:

Directives filtering or extracting from the request

MethodDirectives

These directives filters and extracts routes based on request method.

- *delete*
- *extractMethod*
- *get*
- *head*
- *method*
- *options*
- *overrideMethodWithParameter*
- *patch*

- *post*
- *put*

The structure and way of handling request of all method directives are same. Please see below example

```
val path = pathSingleSlash & (get | put | post |
delete | head | options) & extractMethod

val route =
 path { m =>
   complete(s"Received ${m.name} request!!!")
 }
```

In the above example, if any request comes with a method other than (*get* | *put* | *post* | *delete* | *head* | *options*), it will get rejected.

PathDirectives

List of path directives, available in Akka HTTP:

- *path*
- *pathEnd*
- *pathEndOrSingleSlash*
- *pathPrefix*
- *pathPrefixTest*
- *pathSingleSlash*
- *pathSuffix*
- *pathSuffixTest*
- *rawPathPrefix*
- *rawPathPrefixTest*
- *redirectToNoTrailingSlashIfPresent*
- *redirectToTrailingSlashIfMissing*
- *ignoreTrailingSlash*
- *The PathMatcher DSL*

Some of the most common path directives:

path(pathName): It matches a leading slash followed by pathName and then the end.

path("foo") {
   complete("/foo")
 }

pathEnd: When there is nothing left to match from the path, pathend will be matched. This directive should not be used at the root as the minimal path is the single slash.

pathEnd {
     complete("There is no more path!")
     }

pathPrefix(pathName): It matches a leading slash followed by pathName and then leaves a suffix unmatched.

pathPrefix("foo") {
     pathEnd {
       complete("/bar")
     }
}

pathSingleSlash: It matches when the remaining path is just a single slash.

pathEndOrSingleSlash: It matches either when there is no remaining path or is just a single slash.

HostDirectives

It filters requests based on the hostname part of the Host header contained in incoming requests and extracts its value for usage in inner routes.

extractHost

Extract the hostname part of the Host request header

```
extractHost { hostname =>
  complete(s"Your host is : $hostname")
}
```

host

It has three signatures.

host(hostNames: String*): It rejects all the requests, which have hostname other than passed in the argument.

```
host("abc.com", "xyz.com") {
  complete("Ok")
}
```

host(predicate: String ⇒ Boolean): It rejects all the requests If the hostname does not satisfy the given predicate.

host(regex: Regex): It rejects all the requests If the hostname does not match with the given regular expression.

ParameterDirectives

There are 5 parameter directives in Akka HTTP:

1) *parameter*
2) *parameterMap*
3) *parameterMultiMap*
4) *parameters*
5) *parameterSeq*

- ***parameter***

It simply extracts query parameter value from the request.

```
val route =
 parameter('name) { name =>
    complete(s"Hey '$name' !!")
 }

Get("/?name=Tom") ~> routes ~> check {
 status should === (StatusCodes.OK)

 entityAs[String] should === ("""Hey 'Tom' !!""")
}
```

- ***parameterMap***

If there are multiple parameters in a query, it will extract all parameters in the form of *Map[String, String]* by mapping parameter names to parameter values.

```
val route =
 pathPrefix("register") {
    pathEnd {
      parameterMap { params =>
        complete(s"Hey ! Your name is
${params("name")} and age is ${params("age")}")
      }
    }
```

```
    }
Get("/register?name=Tom&age=26") ~> routes ~> check
{
  status should ===(StatusCodes.OK)

  entityAs[String] should ===("""Hey ! Your name is
Tom and age is 26""")
  }
```

If same parameter name appears more than one time, it will consider the last one as the parameter value. If you still want to catch all parameter values of a parameter name, you can use *parameterMultiMap*.

```
Get("/register?name=Chris&age=28&age=32") ~> routes
~> check {
  status should ===(StatusCodes.OK)

  entityAs[String] should ===("""Hey ! Your name is
Chris and age is 32""")
  }
```

- ***parameterMultiMap***

If there are multiple parameters, appears several times with different value, we can use this directive and it will extract them in the form of *Map[String, List[String]]*.

```
pathPrefix("register") {
  pathEnd {
    parameterMultiMap { params =>
      complete(s"Hey ! Your name is
${params("name")}, age is ${params("age")} and
addresses are ${params("address")}")
    }
  }
}
```

```
}
Get("/register?name=Tom&age=26&address=Chinatown")
~> routes ~> check {
 status should ===(StatusCodes.OK)

 entityAs[String] should ===("""Hey ! Your name is
List(Tom), age is List(26) and addresses are
List(Chinatown)""")
 }

Get("/register?name=Chris&age=28&address=1street&ad
dress=Chinatown") ~> routes ~> check {
 status should ===(StatusCodes.OK)

 entityAs[String] should ===("""Hey ! Your name is
List(Chris), age is List(28) and addresses are
List(1street, Chinatown)""")
 }
```

- ***parameters***

It is similar to parameter directive, the only difference is
that you have the choice to convert query parameters
either into a string or any other type.

parameters("name"): extract value of name as *String*

parameters("name".?): extract value as *Option[String]*

parameters("name" ? "Unknown User"): extract optional
value of name with default value "Unknown User"

parameters("name" ! "Tom"): It requires name to be "Tom"
and extracts nothing.

parameters('name.):* It extraxts all parameter values of
name as Iterable[String]

- ***parameterSeq***

It is similar to *parameters('name.*)* but the only difference is that it maintains the original order.

To start with Akka HTTP directives, above information is sufficient. Since Akka HTTP provides a good list of parameter directives, you can go to the official documentation ***https://doc.akka.io/docs/akka-http/current/scala/http/routing-dsl/directives/by-trait.htm**l* to understand each directive in details.

Chapter 9: WebSocket Support

HTTP is a uni-directional protocol where a request is always initiated by the client, server processes and returns a response, and then the client consumes it. *WebSocket* is a bi-directional protocol where there are no pre-defined message patterns such as request/response. Either client or server can send a message to the other party.
. If we have the scenario to transfer real-time data from and to the server over an HTTP connection, we use WebSocket.

In most cases, WebSocket channel runs through an upgraded HTTP/s connection.

Websockets allow sending data both sides, but only one message can be open per direction of the WebSocket connection. And because message size is not known, the data of the message is represented as a stream. In Akka HTTP, the basic unit of data exchange in the WebSocket protocol is represented by *Message* trait.

Data can either be a binary message or a text message and are represented by *BinaryMessage* and *TextMessage*. *Message* is a supertype of both classes. Both of these subtypes also have their own Strict subclasses that contain raw data (String or ByteString) which is a natural choice for sending completely assembled messages.

```
sealed trait Message extends
```

```
akka.http.javadsl.model.ws.Message

sealed trait TextMessage extends
akka.http.javadsl.model.ws.TextMessage with Message
{
  /**
   * The contents of this message as a stream.
   */
  def textStream: Source[String, _]

  /** Java API */
  override def getStreamedText:
javadsl.Source[String, _] = textStream.asJava
  override def asScala: TextMessage = this
}

sealed trait BinaryMessage extends
akka.http.javadsl.model.ws.BinaryMessage with
Message {
  /**
   * The contents of this message as a stream.
   */
  def dataStream: Source[ByteString, _]

  /** Java API */
  override def getStreamedData:
javadsl.Source[ByteString, _] = dataStream.asJava
  override def asScala: BinaryMessage = this
}
```

When an akka-http server receives a message in one part
through a WebSocket stream, it tries to bundle the data as
an instance of the Strict class. If a message is incomplete
and the length is unknown, we should consider it as a
streamed message and handle accordingly.

Low-level Implementation

Akka HTTP provides low level and high level web socket
support. For upgrading your connection to websocket, your
implementation should include

akka.http.scaladsl.model.ws.UpgradeToWebsocket
header in every initial request. If the Server gets request
with such header, connection is able to upgrade to a
websocket connection. *UpgradeToWebsocket* also
handles Handshaking, but it's well hidden in the application
and don't need to be managed manually.

After accepting websocket request, it can respond by its
handleMessages method.

Let's see below low level websocket sample:

```
def chatService(name: String) =
  Flow[Message]
    .mapConcat {
      case tm: TextMessage =>
TextMessage(Source.single(name + "::") ++
tm.textStream) :: Nil
    }

val requestHandler: HttpRequest => HttpResponse = {
  case req @ HttpRequest(GET, Uri.Path("/chat"), _,
_, _) =>
    req.header[UpgradeToWebSocket] match {
      case Some(upgrade) => {

upgrade.handleMessages(chatService(req.uri.query().
getOrElse("name", "")))
      }
      case None => HttpResponse(400, entity = "Not a
valid websocket request!")
    }
}
```

If *UpgradeToWebsocket* header is found, it is used to
generate a response by passing a handler for WebSocket
messages to the *handleMessages* method. If no such
header is found a 400 Bad Request response is
generated.

High Level Implementation

If we are using high-level routing DSL, we have to use *handleWebSocketMessages* directive, which will upgrade connections to websockets. Let's see an example

```scala
def route =
  path("chat") {
    parameter('name) { name =>
      handleWebSocketMessages(broadcast(name))
    }
  }

def broadcast(name: String): Flow[Message, Message,
Any] = {
  Flow[Message].mapConcat {
    case tm: TextMessage =>
      TextMessage(Source.single(name + "::") ++
tm.textStream) :: Nil
  }
}
```

akka-http under the hood uses akka-streams for data processing. below is an example to test web socket request using mock WebSocket probe.

```scala
"Websocket" should {
  "be able to pull and push message" in {
    val wsClient = WSProbe()
    WS("/chat?name=Chris", wsClient.flow) ~> route
~>
      check {
        isWebSocketUpgrade shouldEqual true

        wsClient.sendMessage("How are you?")
        wsClient.expectMessage("Chris::How are
you?")
      }
  }
}
```

You can find complete example here
https://gist.github.com/ayushmishra2005/1bbace9de59 **3811849a810752e601505** .

If you are planning to create any websocket based microservice architecure, you can follow one of my blog *https://blog.knoldus.com/2016/08/08/a-simple-example-of-websocket-based-microservice-architecure-using-akka-http-in-scala/*

Chapter 10: Rejection Handler

While filtering directives to handling one specific type of request, if the filtering conditions are not met, a rejection occurs. If there are multiple routes and the first route does not match, it will continue searching matching route through the routing structure and possibly find another route that can complete it.

Let's see an example

```scala
lazy val employeeRoutes: Route =
  Route.seal(pathPrefix("employees") {
    pathEnd {
      get {
        complete(list)
      } ~
        post {
          entity(as[Employee]) { employee =>
            list = list.copy(employees =
list.employees ++ Seq(employee))
            log.info("Created employee :",
employee.name)
            complete((StatusCodes.Created,
employee))
          }
        }
    }
  })

//Test-case

"EmployeeRoutes" should {
  val testData =
    Table(
      ("clue", "path", "expectedStatus",
"expectedEntity"),
      ("return employee list", Get("/employees"),
StatusCodes.OK,  """{"employees":[]}"""),
      ("add an employee", Post("/employees",
Employee("1", "John")),  StatusCodes.Created,
"""{"id":"1","name":"John"}"""),
```

```
      ("reject the request, if respective resource
is not found",           Get("/emp"),
StatusCodes.NotFound, "The requested resource could
not be found."),
      ("reject the request, if the requests content-
type is unsupported", Post("/employees", ""),
StatusCodes.UnsupportedMediaType,
      "The request's Content-Type is not
supported. Expected:\napplication/json")
    )
 forAll(testData) { case (clue, path,
expectedStatus, expectedEntity) =>
    s"$clue" in {
      path ~> routes ~> check {
        status should ===(expectedStatus)

        entityAs[String] should ===(expectedEntity)
      }
    }
  }
}
```

In above example,

1) When we hit any random route, it rejects the request but rejection list is still empty. rejections is a list of rejection. If there are more rejections all of them will be picked up and collected.

According to Akka HTTP documentation "*Empty Rejections signals that a request was not handled because the respective resource could not be found. Akka HTTP reserves the special status of "empty rejection" to this most common failure a service is likely to produce.*"

Route.seal() internally wraps its argument route with the **handleRejections** directive in order to "catch" and handle any rejection.

2) If we hit correct route with invalid body content, it gives *UnsupportedRequestContentTypeRejection.*

Akka HTTP comes with a set of predefined rejections, which are used by the many predefined directives.

If you don't want to display rejection output like "requested resource could not be found", Akka HTTP also provides a way to customize rejections. Let's modify example:

```scala
lazy val employeeRoutes: Route =
  Route.seal(pathPrefix("employees") {
    pathEnd {
      get {
        complete(list)
      } ~
        post {
          entity(as[Employee]) { employee =>
            list = list.copy(employees =
list.employees ++ Seq(employee))
            log.info("Created employee :",
employee.name)
            complete((StatusCodes.Created,
employee))
          }
        }
    }
  })

//Test-case

"EmployeeRoutes" should {
  val rejectData =
    Table(
      ("clue", "path", "expected"),
      ("reject the request, if respective resource
is not found", Get("/emp"), Nil)        )
```

```scala
 forAll(rejectData) { case (clue, path, expected)
=>
   s"$clue" in {
     path ~> routes ~> check {
       status should ===(StatusCodes.NotFound)
       entityAs[String] should
===("""{"code":404,"type":"NotFound","message":"The
requested resource could not be found. Go to
abc.com."}""")
     }
   }
 }
}
```

Chapter 11: Client-Side API Implementation

Akka HTTP offers capabilities to consume remote HTTP services by the ***akka-http-core*** module. The Akka HTTP client API uses the same abstractions as the HTTP server API.

The HTTP client API is divided into three levels of abstraction:

Request-Level Client-Side API

It is the recommended for most use cases and most convenient way of using Akka HTTP's client-side functionality. However, it internally uses *Host-Level Client-Side API* to get a response from the server. For a quick start to know how Akka HTTP client side API works, you can start with this API. However, this API is not recommended for long-running requests because It is implemented on top of a connection pool that is shared inside the actor system.

Let's see an example

1) Create Akka HTTP server-side API

```
trait EmployeeRoutes extends JsonSupport {
  implicit def system: ActorSystem

  lazy val log = Logging(system,
classOf[EmployeeRoutes])

  var list: Employees = Employees(Nil)

  implicit lazy val timeout = Timeout(5.seconds)
```

```
lazy val employeeRoutes: Route =
  Route.seal(pathPrefix("employees") {
    pathEnd {
      get {
        complete(list)
      } ~
      post {
        entity(as[Employee]) { employee =>
          list = list.copy(employees =
list.employees ++ Seq(employee))
          log.info("Created employee :",
employee.name)
          complete((StatusCodes.Created,
employee))
        }
      }
    }
  })
}
```

Find the complete code here:

*https://gist.github.com/ayushmishra2005/7f159b57f14a
14afe6a34f1ffee20383*

Now create Akka HTTP server

```
object ServerStarter extends App with
EmployeeRoutes {
 implicit val system = ActorSystem("my-system")
 implicit val materializer = ActorMaterializer()
 implicit val executionContext = system.dispatcher

 val (host, port) = ("localhost", 8080)
 val bindingFuture: Future[ServerBinding] =
   Http().bindAndHandle(employeeRoutes, host, port)

 log.info(s"Server online at
http://localhost:8080/\nPress RETURN to stop...")
 bindingFuture.failed.foreach { ex =>
   log.error(ex, "Failed to bind to {}:{}!", host,
port)
```

```
  }
}
```

2) Create Akka HTTP client-side API

```scala
object Client extends App{
  implicit val system = ActorSystem()
  implicit val materializer = ActorMaterializer()
  implicit val executionContext = system.dispatcher

  val responseFuture: Future[HttpResponse] =
Http().singleRequest(HttpRequest(uri =
"http://localhost:8080/employees"))

  responseFuture
    .onComplete {
      case Success(res) => Console.out.println(res)
      case Failure(_)   => sys.error("something
wrong with requested url!")
    }
}
```

To run this example, you have to start server and client on two separate JVMs.

Host-Level Client-Side API

Using this API, you can manage a connection-pool to one specific host/port endpoint.

Connection-Level Client-Side API

It is recommended only for specific use cases, where you want full control of HTTP connections.

One Last Thing...

George Bernard Shaw Quote: *"If you teach a man anything, he will never learn."*

We learn by doing. If you have gone through all chapters, you will be able to start building microservices in Akka HTTP right away. Microservices are the next best thing in modern software architecture and development. The use of microservices in application development is on the rise. This is because, with microservices, software development processes are made much easy and faster. The developer can focus on what they do best. Microservices are easy to deploy in a production environment since they are made up of very small subcomponents.

Microservices adhere to a core tenet of the UNIX platform to "do one thing and do it well".

There are numerous ways to implement microservices. The best choice depends on what you find easiest and the most familiar. Take the knowledge from this book and use it to build microservices using Akka HTTP with Scala. We recommend that developers should employ the concept of microservices whenever they are developing their applications according to their use cases.

A lot of this discussion is already preached by our partner Lightbend, in their webinars.

Before start working on Microservices, we strongly recommend you to read this blog: Wait! Don't write your microservice ... yet, written by Mr. Vikas Hazrati, CEO and

CTO of Knoldus Inc.

You can also go through below blogs, written by Knoldus, to have a deep understanding of Microservices and Akka HTTP.

Please find below some sample projects, which you can use as a template:

https://github.com/knoldus/akka-http-contact-management
https://github.com/knoldus/cockroach-akka-http-starter-kit.g8
https://github.com/knoldus/angular2-akka-http-scala-todo
https://github.com/knoldus/simple-akka-http-websocket-example.g8
https://github.com/knoldus/akka-http-websocket-microservices.g8
https://github.com/knoldus/scala-solr-akkahttp.g8
https://github.com/knoldus/neo4j-scala-akkahttp.g8

https://github.com/knoldus/spark-akka-http-couchbase-starter-kit.g8
https://github.com/knoldus/akka-http-slick.g8
https://github.com/knoldus/akka-http-multipart-form-data.g8
https://github.com/knoldus/akka-http-JanusGraph
https://github.com/knoldus/akka-http-swagger
https://github.com/knoldus/spark-akka-http
https://github.com/knoldus/jwt-akka-http-example
https://github.com/knoldus/akka-http-file-upload

Here is the link of all gists, which I have mentioned on this book:

https://gist.github.com/ayushmishra2005

This should be enough to get you started with building microservices! You can email or write to let me know what you did or didn't like about this book.

E-mail: *ayush@knoldus.com*
LinkedIn: *https://www.linkedin.com/in/ayush-mishra-a2787b23/*
Twitter: *ayushmishra2005*
Github: *https://github.com/knoldus*
Blogs: *https://blog.knoldus.com/author/ayushmishra2005/*

This book is part of Knoldus Reactive Programming Series. To check video tutorial, please go to **knolx.knoldus.com** . For more information, please go to www.knoldus.com .

Hope you enjoyed reading. If you are interested in a fulfilling career in software craftsmanship then please send a mail to jobs@knoldus.com. Please visit our website www.knoldus.com for more details.

Thank you again for reading my ebook. If you found it useful, please leave us a review when you bought the book. Thanks again!

Ayush Kumar Mishra

www.ingramcontent.com/pod-product-compliance
Lightning Source LLC
Chambersburg PA
CBHW031247050326
40690CB00007B/991